MENTAL HEALTH & WELL-BEING ACTIVITIES

RESILIENCE

COPING STRATEGIES

MENTAL HEALTH & WELL-BEING ACTIVITIES

RESILIENCE

COPING STRATEGIES

STEPHANIE GEORGE & ANKE BAUER

LOGGERHEAD
PUBLISHING

WWW.LOGGERHEADPUBLISHING.CO.UK

First published in 2018 by

Loggerhead Publishing Ltd, PO Box 928, Northampton NN7 9AP, United Kingdom
Tel: 01604 870828
International Tel: +44 (0) 1604 870828
Fax: 01604 870986
International Fax: +44 (0) 1604 870986
www.loggerheadpublishing.co.uk

Printed in the United Kingdom

Design and artwork by Moo Creative (Luton)

British Library Cataloguing in Publication Data. A catalogue record for this book is available from the British Library

ISBN 978-1-909380-05-9

Contents

About the authors

Stephanie George MA is a Deputy Head teacher in London. She has been responsible for the training of over 1500 pastoral staff for the past 20 years through her work as a national trainer for Osiris Educational. She wrote the first text book on Learning Mentor policy and practice in the United Kingdom in 2010, *The Learning Mentor Manual*, Sage Publications and has since published a further seven books: *Activities for Mentoring Young People* (2013), *Activities to Help Young People Deal with Anger* (2014), *Activities to Help Young People Deal with Bullying* (co-authored, 2014), *Activities to Help Young People Deal with Stress & Anxiety (*2015), *The Mentoring Toolkit* (2016), *Activities to Help Young People Deal with Decisions and Choices* (co-authored, 2016), *Activities to Help Young People Build Character* (co-authored, 2017) as well as two *Talking Boxes* (2015) of discussion cards on attendance/punctuality and moral dilemmas, all for Loggerhead Publishing. Stephanie also developed the first baseline assessment model to measure the impact of mentoring for individual students.

In 2013 Stephanie was recognised by the Times Educational Supplement for her outstanding work in leading mentoring teams and received a TES Award for 2013. In 2015 she received a Pearson Teaching Award.

Anke Bauer BA is a social worker in a secondary school in southern Germany. In the past she worked as a learning mentor in secondary schools in London. With her background in European Social Work, Ecology and Ceramics she is mainly working in whole class settings using elements of experiential education.

Acknowledgements

From Stephanie

I have known Anke for almost two decades. As I write now in 2018, this really does feel like yesterday. Writing a book is never easy but this one has been a joy to write with Anke as we see how far our initial ideas and interventions have positively impacted upon the children and young people we have worked with.

Thank you to Sue East, Sue Rosner, Jeba Begum, Jane Chesters, Pamela Alexander, Kalash Thakor, Patricia Andrews and Bushra Nasir whose supportive words and selfless deeds have touched me over the last 20 years. Women like you are one in a million.

Love to my Gracie.

From Anke

Thank you to Tibor Schneider, an experienced pedagogue, who is an inspiration for my work and helped me develop some of the ideas in this book. I am fortunate to have you as a colleague.

To Elias, Maria, Samuel and Emma for their patience with mummy writing on her book.

Thank you to my husband for his faith in me – and proofreading and looking after our children.

From us both

Our gratitude and appreciation must go to Catherine McAllister, our publisher, and to Sue Christelow for her editorial brilliance.

Introduction

Staff working in schools face a multitude of issues in addition to teaching and learning; some of these issues include social, emotional and mental health issues. Mental health issues are a social and public concern and the government has a made a commitment to mental health services and provision in schools.

Moves are afoot to ensure that every primary and secondary school in England and Wales has staff trained in mental health first aid and are given a single point of contact with local mental health services. Children and young people will be taught more about mental health, including keeping safe online and cyber-bullying.

This book on resilience coping strategies is the first in a Mental Health & Well-Being Series providing practical activities to help practitioners when working with children and young people in schools.

This resource provides 20 activities including:

- Early help assessment tools
- Action plans
- Assessment matrices
- Social learning themes to help contextualise student experiences
- Signposting tools

This book is intended for use by those working in a variety of settings including schools, alternative education settings, Learning Support Units, Pupil/Student Referral Units, Isolation Units, Exclusion Rooms, youth clubs, community groups and similar settings. The book can be used with students from the ages of 10 in the upper primary phase through to the upper secondary phase of 18 years of age depending upon ability and need.

The activities can be led by teachers, learning mentors, behaviour mentors, pastoral team leaders and assistants, exclusion room staff, HLTAs, special educational needs staff, family support workers and members of welfare teams.

Within this book are 20 resilience-focused activities that cross the bridge between the pastoral and curriculum aspects of learning.

Best practice tells us that a holistic and all-encompassing view of the student is paramount and the pastoral and curriculum aspects of learning should have synergy. We only have to look at the outcomes of the most successful schools to observe this. One without the other does not serve the needs of our young people well. This book is about the whole student.

The activities can be used in mentoring sessions, small group sessions, circle time, one-to-one sessions and PCSHE lessons.

The resources and activities in this book aim to help you to help the young people that you are working with by ultimately focusing upon one thing – their progress.

Resilience

The building of resilience, development of a growth mind-set, the reference to a solution focused mind-set, grit, bouncebackability are the buzzwords we hear within the educational landscape of the early twenty-first century. However, these phrases can sometimes become platitudinal responses to real concerns such as the endemic use of social media that threatens the very joy and innocence of childhood yet is lauded as technological advancement.

In actuality the need to build resilience and to be resilient to life's turbulence has always been present. Some call it emotional literacy, some call it emotional intelligence and some call it grit. Whatever we call it we know it when we see it. We know that when there is turmoil, chaos, instability and disquiet we look within ourselves for that which keeps us steady. It is this quality within any child, any adult, anybody that we hope to see in order to steady ourselves and emerge from instability with a surefootedness and step and know that we can move forward. It is this that we wish to cultivate and it is this that we explore within this book.

This book is about:

- Identifying Resilience

- Building Resilience

- Supporting Resilience

Should you have any concerns about a young person that you are working with please seek further specialist advice. Please follow the safeguarding procedures of the organisation within which you work.

How to use this book

We want this book to give you and us as practitioners a range of resources that can be used during interventions, when opening the conversation becomes too challenging, when you need to be able to DO something and the young person needs help right now.

You can use these resources one to one, in small groups and in a workshop and/or larger groups. A workbook is provided at the end of the book to track the use of each activity so as to assist with evaluation; this is also a useful resource for providing feedback and evidence of the working intervention as this is what these resources are. In addition it offers an opportunity for self-reflection for the student.

The activities are structured in the following way:

1. Activity Objective

2. Intended Audience

3. Context

4. Activity Instructions

5. Closing the Activity

All of the activities have accompanying activity sheets, which are numbered. The activities can be used discretely as stand-alone tasks.

At the very heart of this book is a set of activities that enable practitioners to demonstrate the impact of intervention.

Most importantly, the activities, once complete, will provide you with evidence of work with students that is demonstrable to them and at the same time provides evidence for other stakeholders in your setting be they parents, governors, leadership teams or Ofsted.

Mental Health – What is it?

Activity Objective

To give students the opportunity to engage in dialogue around the term 'Mental Health'.

Intended Audience

Individual or small groups

Context

Positive Mental Health is a fundamental part of a young person's development. This activity examines the term Mental Health and what it may mean.

Activity Instructions

1)   Ask the student(s) to discuss what they believe the term 'Mental Health' might mean.

2)   Ask the student(s) to jot down their ideas, using Activity Sheet 1.

3)   There are thought prompts that can be used for the student(s) but do not reveal these until they have generated some of their own ideas – see Activity Sheet 2.

4)   Encourage the student(s) to discuss and then decide which of those ideas on Activity Sheet 2 would be their highest ranking concerns about Mental Health and note these in Activity Sheet 3 in the boxes.

5)   Explore with the student(s) their reasons for the order that they have given and reflect upon whether their understanding of Mental Health has changed since the start of the session.

Closing the Activity

Draw the activity to a close by summing up the steps completed and students' understanding.
Do ensure you give time for any queries or concerns with this sensitive area.

Mental Health Thought Shower

Thought Prompts

Fear	Afraid	Dread
Anxiety	Panic	Crazy
Weird	Strange	Charity
Eccentric	Sick	Unwell
Mad	Unapproachable	Sensitive

My Concerns about Mental Health

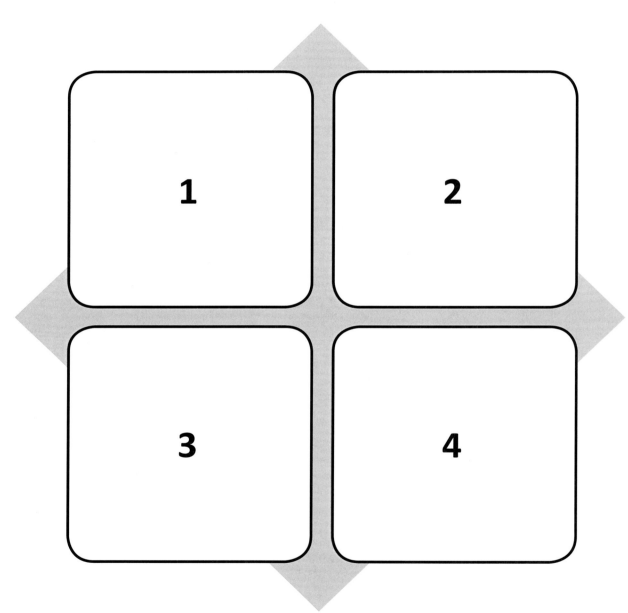

Building Resilience Initial Self-Assessment

Activity Objective

To give students the opportunity to assess themselves in order to provide a baseline for measuring progress with a focus on resilience.

Intended Audience

Individual

Context

The key thing here is to obtain the student's opinion about their own progress, promoting ownership for the student of that progress to enable action planning to be specific, measurable, achievable, realistic and time focused.

Activity Instructions

1. Allow the student time to work through the Initial Self-Assessment Form (Activity Sheet 4).
2. Review the form and assessment scores as a basis for discussion and ascertaining whether the student has a preference for which aspect of the assessment needs addressing as a priority.

Closing the Activity

Close the activity by logging the evidence in the Student Feedback and Tracking Workbook and moving on to the SMART Action Planning activity in this book.

Initial Self-Assessment Form – Building Resilience

Please circle one box which best describes you. 1 is low and 10 is high											
Name of Student										Form	
Mentor										Date	
	Descriptor	Rating scale = 1 is low and 10 is high.									Descriptor
1.	Insensitive	1	2	3	4	5	6	7	8	9	10	Sensitive
2.	Impatient	1	2	3	4	5	6	7	8	9	10	Patient
3.	Unstable	1	2	3	4	5	6	7	8	9	10	Stable
4.	Insular	1	2	3	4	5	6	7	8	9	10	Open
5.	Controlling	1	2	3	4	5	6	7	8	9	10	Sharing
6.	Impatient	1	2	3	4	5	6	7	8	9	10	Patient
7.	Easily influenced	1	2	3	4	5	6	7	8	9	10	Impartial
8.	Unreliable	1	2	3	4	5	6	7	8	9	10	Reliable
9.	Subjective	1	2	3	4	5	6	7	8	9	10	Objective
Totals – Add up all the scores											Add all scores in the columns and enter below score out of 90

Building Resilience Action Plan

Activity Objective

To develop a set of SMART targets and create a plan of action following completion of the resilience assessment.

Intended Audience

Individual

Context

Best practice in mentoring requires target setting and action planning with the student as the student needs to plan how he/she will make progress and what needs to be done to get there. The action plan should have SMART features, i.e. it should be Specific, Measurable, Achievable, Realistic and Time focused.

Activity Instructions

1. Using Activity Sheet 5 begin a discussion around target setting with the student looking at the flow chart and steps therein. A focused discussion about the issues affecting learning and achievement needs to take place.

2. Having had a discussion with the student and developed an area to work on, it is time to set a target and create a plan of action. The plan on Activity Sheet 6 includes the following elements:

a) Specific – What does the student wish to achieve?

b) Measurable – How will the student know that the goal has been achieved? (What evidence will be seen?)

c) Achievable – Does the student have the capacity/resources to do this? How will the student achieve this?

d) Realistic – Is the goal actually achievable and credible?

e) Time Focused – When does the student wish to achieve this?

The plan should now be SMART.

Closing the Activity

Review the plan with the student, make any changes to the draft and then finalise the plan. Praise the student; he/she should now get ready for progress.

Agree a review date at which you will revisit the plan.

5 Activity Sheet

A Plan of Action

Specific
What does the student wish
to achieve?

Measurable
How will the student know that
the goal has been achieved?
(What evidence will be seen?)

Achievable
Does the student have the
capacity/resources to do this?
How will the student achieve this?

Realistic
Is the goal actually
achievable, manageable and
practicable?

Time Focused
When does the student
wish to achieve this?
What is the time frame for
accomplishment?

6 Activity Sheet

Building Resilience SMART Action Plan

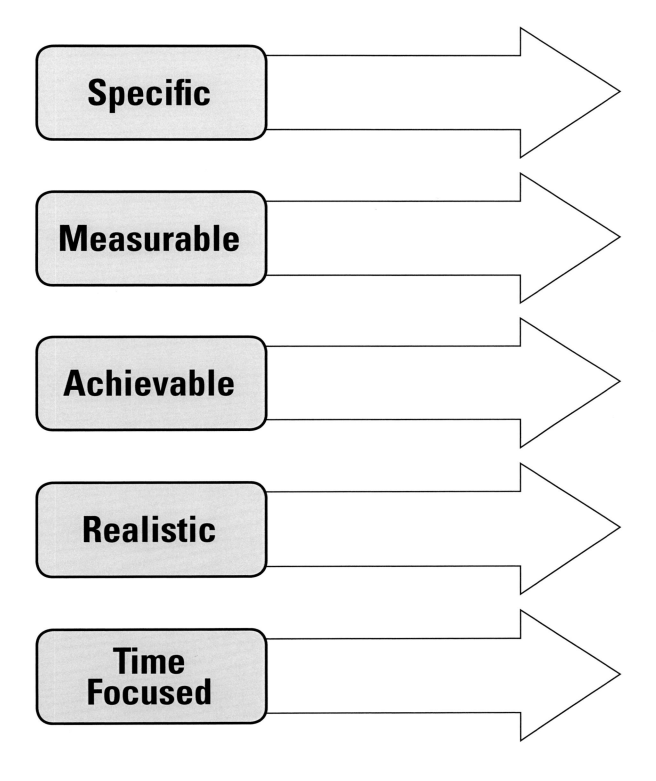

Specific

Measurable

Achievable

Realistic

Time Focused

Building Resilience Reassessment

Activity Objective

To give students the opportunity to reassess themselves in order to provide a baseline for measuring progress.

Intended Audience

Individual

Context

This reassessment activity should be undertaken at the end of or at suitable intervals during the mentoring process. The Resilience 'Initial Self-Assessment' activity should always have been completed first as your baseline assessment of the student

The reassessment seeks to establish the difference mentoring has made in a data-driven and quantifiable way. You may find that you need to conduct the action plan again should there be any areas where there is concern or no movement.

Activity Instructions

1. The student completes the Reassessment Form (Activity Sheet 7).

   The questions will be familiar, having undertaken the original Initial Self-Assessment Form previously.

2. Provide the Reassessment Form to the student and allow adequate time to reflect upon responses and then complete it.

3. Once completed move to the next activity to evaluate the differences between the initial assessment and the reassessment.

4. Once again be mindful of the issues surrounding mental health and refer the matter to appropriate safeguarding staff should there be any concern at all.

Closing the Activity

Record the completion of the reassessment in the Student Tracking and Evaluation Workbook.

Building Resilience Reassessment Form

Please circle one box which best describes you. 1 is low and 10 is high											
Name of Student										**Form**	
Mentor										**Date**	
	Descriptor	**Rating scale = 1 is low and 10 is high.**									**Descriptor**
1.	Insensitive	1	2	3	4	5	6	7	8	9	10	Sensitive
2.	Impatient	1	2	3	4	5	6	7	8	9	10	Patient
3.	Unstable	1	2	3	4	5	6	7	8	9	10	Stable
4.	Insular	1	2	3	4	5	6	7	8	9	10	Open
5.	Controlling	1	2	3	4	5	6	7	8	9	10	Sharing
6.	Impatient	1	2	3	4	5	6	7	8	9	10	Patient
7.	Easily influenced	1	2	3	4	5	6	7	8	9	10	Impartial
8.	Unreliable	1	2	3	4	5	6	7	8	9	10	Reliable
9.	Subjective	1	2	3	4	5	6	7	8	9	10	Objective
Totals – Add up all the scores											Add all scores in the columns and enter below score out of 90

Building Resilience Evaluation

Activity Objective

The aim of this activity is to assess, evaluate and then reflect upon the progress made at the start of the intervention with the young person and now, at a periodic interval with regard to resilience, and any developments we can review, mark and work on further.

Intended Audience

Individual

Context

The time is now here to look at what difference the intervention has made and whether there has been any tangible progress. The key thing here is to obtain the student's opinion about their own progress, promoting ownership for the student of that progress to enable the next phase of action planning and target setting to be specific, measurable, achievable, realistic and time focused.

Activity Instructions

1. You will need the initial Self-Assessment Form (taken from the activity 'Initial Self-Assessment') completed, plus the Reassessment Form completed.

2. Now look at The Assessment Evaluation Form (Activity Sheet 8).

You will need to map the responses for each of the forms onto the Assessment Evaluation Form. You will need to calculate the differences (+ or -). Calculate the total responses for each category. What you will then have is the difference for each category as a negative or a positive improvement.

Closing the Activity

Review the gains and losses for each area and move towards a second action plan for progress if appropriate and necessary.

Building Resilience - Assessment Evaluation Form

Name of Student			Form
Question number	BASELINE RATING This number score taken from the initial Self-Assessment Form	REASSESSMENT RATING This number score taken when assessment is conducted after a period of intervention	DIFFERENCE (+/-)
1.			
2.			
3.			
4.			
5.			
6.			
7.			
8.			
9.			
Totals: Add up totals to see overall score to enable the student to see plus or minus gains or deficit.			

Resilient, Really? Me?

Activity Objective

To give students the opportunity to assess how resilient they are.

Intended Audience

Individual

Context

When the objective is to strengthen resilience in students it is good to know the areas that they are still working on. Then future activities can be chosen accordingly.

Activity Instructions

1. The student completes the questionnaire on Activity Sheet 9. The totals are first added up in each line and then added up to give a total.

2. Activity Sheet 10 is then used to evaluate the questionnaire. There are three categories. Talk about which category the student is in and what he/she thinks about it.

Closing the Activity

As a last step look at the questionnaire again and make a plan together with the student about what he/she wants to look at more closely in the next sessions.

9 Activity Sheet

Complete the questionnaire by ticking the box that applies to you - from 1 'No, not at all' to 5 'Yes, totally agree'.

	No, not at all ---> Yes, totally agree				
I do well in challenging situations	1	2	3	4	5
I look more to the future than to the past	1	2	3	4	5
I do well under pressure, e.g. before a test	1	2	3	4	5
I enjoy life, no matter how well I feel today	1	2	3	4	5
I focus on solutions, rather than problems	1	2	3	4	5
I am flexible when there is a change of plans	1	2	3	4	5
When facing a problem I analyse the facts and I don't panic	1	2	3	4	5
I am happy to risk that I may fail if I am trying new things	1	2	3	4	5
I accept that stress, failures and sadness are normal situations in life	1	2	3	4	5
I have lots of people supporting me in my community	1	2	3	4	5
I can easily empathise with other people and relate to their feelings	1	2	3	4	5
I regularly take time to meet with friends	1	2	3	4	5
I have at least one good friend with whom I can be how I really am and share joy and sadness	1	2	3	4	5
I enjoy being out in nature	1	2	3	4	5
I am often the first one to offer help to teachers or other students	1	2	3	4	5
I have people who inspire me	1	2	3	4	5
I quickly get help and advice when I need it	1	2	3	4	5
I have a good sense of humour and can laugh at my own mistakes	1	2	3	4	5
I often pause and feel thankful, even for little things	1	2	3	4	5
I am good at improvising	1	2	3	4	5

continued over

I am generally a very happy person	1	2	3	4	5
I expect that solutions can be found and continue working on a difficult situation	1	2	3	4	5
I like meeting new people and making new experiences	1	2	3	4	5
I don't compare myself to others who are smarter, faster etc than me, because I know that I give my best	1	2	3	4	5
I like getting feedback from others and try to learn from it	1	2	3	4	5
I am good at looking after myself and I am my best friend	1	2	3	4	5
Totals in each line					
Total number of points					

Activity Sheet

Category A

26 – 66 points

Well done for starting to look at how well you cope with stress and difficult situations. Buckle up, you are about to begin an exciting journey.

The assessment is showing that you find it difficult to work under pressure. Maybe you are easily frightened by situations out of your comfort zone. When being criticised you sometimes feel helpless. Ask yourself: Do I want to learn to deal with challenges more confidently? Yes? Then that is a sure sign you are ready to work on strengthening your resilience muscle.

Category B

67 – 99 points

You have already developed good skills in caring for how you feel. You are often in touch with yourself and your community.

Continue to look after your feelings and continue to work further towards a strong self-esteem. Take on board the advice you get in the next sessions. In some areas you still need help with growing stronger. Look at them more closely together with the adult working with you and continue on your journey.

Category C

100 – 130 points

Wow, you are doing well in dealing with difficulties. You stay in touch with your values and are happy to stick up for what you believe in.

You have already gained a lot of inner strength and bouncing back from times of pressure isn't hard for you. Where there are still areas that can be developed further work on them and you will come out strong and ready to face the challenges that come your way.

Giving Gifts

Activity Objective

To give students the opportunity to become aware of their personal resources.

Intended Audience

Individual, pairs, small groups to whole classes

Context

In this activity the students work in pairs or groups if possible. The activity works well even with whole school classes. The students have to know each other though. For young people getting positive feedback from peers is a very powerful tool to raise their self-esteem. The students get a picture of their abilities and what they are good at.

Activity Instructions

1. Give each student a copy of Activity Sheet 11. They start by making the face outline their own – colouring the eyes, skin, adding hair etc.

2. If working with an individual student fill in Activity Sheet 11 together with the student. Ask the student to write good qualities and abilities around their face. You might need to prompt him/her and point out good qualities and abilities that you see as their mentor.

    If working with pairs, let the students exchange their sheets and give each other positive feedback.

    With groups let the students leave their paper on their desks or - what I prefer - on the floor if you have the space. Ask them to go round freely with a pencil and write positive feedback around their peers' faces.

3. The students take their faces home after the activity. For referring to the activity in the future you can photocopy the sheet first and keep the copy in the student's file.

Closing the Activity

Thank the students for their openness and willingness to give and receive feedback. Remind them that they have a lot of personal resources that they draw on when facing challenges.

11 **Activity Sheet**

Student Name:

... is able to   ... has learnt to

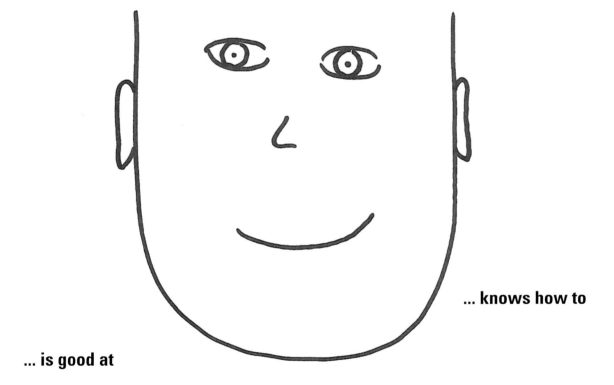

... knows how to

... is good at

... can

Help! My Community of Helpers

Activity Objective

To raise awareness of the student's community resources.

Intended Audience

Individual, pairs, small groups.

Context

Resilience is best developed within the context of a strong community. Young people ideally grow up being supported by a network of people, their wider family, their faith community, neighbours etc. Sometimes students are either not aware of their existing community around them or they just aren't familiar with the helpers available. With this activity they can be pointed towards people who are already there, and whose help and advice they can access in future.

Activity Instructions

1. Talk about situations when the student(s) might need help from other people in the community. Think about school, health professionals, faith and community, about feeling sad or stressed. Who is helping me? Where do I go when I am sad? What do I do when I feel stressed? Find out who can help you with … in your community/school! So next time you need help you know where to go.

2. Ask the student(s) to fill in Activity Sheet 12 – a mind map of the network of community resources that the student(s) can access. You can add more bubbles if you find more sources of help for the student(s) in their community.

Closing the Activity

Having found out about their network of helpers around them stress to the student(s) the importance of being part of this network. They play an active part in it – receiving help and advice is one side, being helpful towards others – the elderly or younger children – is the other side. It feels great to be part of a lively, caring community.

12 Activity Sheet

Help! My Network

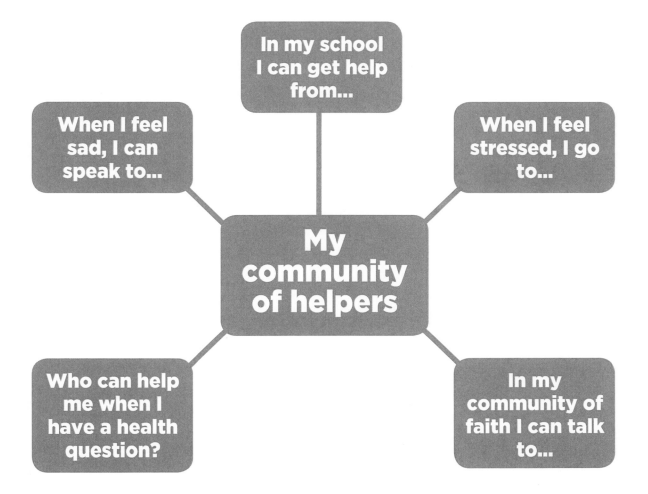

Train Your Resilience Muscle

Activity Objective

For students to practise acting assertively. Typical situations that young people face at home or school are being used in a role-play setting.

Intended Audience

Small groups and groups up to class size

Context

There are many situations where young people need to take a stand in their everyday life. It can be difficult for them to stay authentic and to stick to their own opinions and values. This activity allows the students to practise acting in an assertive way in a safe setting. Using role-play situations they are able to exercise their resilience muscle, so it is easier to face the next real-life challenge without fear.

Activity Instructions

1. In preparation for this activity, photocopy Activity Sheet 13. There are three different situations. Each situation has two characters: A and B. Cut out the 6 boxes, so that each student gets only A or B of one of the three situations. If your group has more than six students make more copies and you will have some of the pairs acting out the same situation.

2. Ask the students to use all the space in the room. Each pair now enacts their situation, allowing about five minutes for the role-play. The pairs all act out at the same time at this point. This is their practice run.

3. Next come together as a whole group and ask each pair to role-play their situation.

4. Depending on the time you have and the size of your group, you can either pause for reflection after each pair, or let them all enact their role-play and reflect at the end.

5. You can use the following questions for reflection:

    -   How did you feel when acting this out?

    -   What options did you consider?

    -   Did you choose the most assertive option?

    -   Which helpful things did you or could you say to yourself in your mind that would strengthen you in the situation?

Closing the Activity

Draw the activity to a close by asking the students to visualise how they want to approach future challenging situations. If they do this regularly they can also train for real-life situations.

At the end read out this quote from Reinhold Niebuhr as a final thought for the students to take with them:

"Grant me the serenity to accept the things I cannot change,

Courage to change the things I can,

And wisdom to know the difference."

Train Your Resilience Muscle - Role-play Suggestions

Situation 1 **Character A** Your teacher assigned you a seat next to a student, Ben, who you don't like. You wanted to sit next to your friend. You feel punished. You know last week you have talked more in class than you should have. You talk to the teacher.	**Situation 1** **Character B** One of your students, Ben, has been playing up a lot in class lately. He needs someone with a calm attitude next to him. You choose A because you know that he/she will have a positive influence on Ben.
Situation 2 **Character A** You want to go out to the cinema with a friend and need permission from your parent. You think you have been quite good recently, bringing out the rubbish and helping with clearing the dinner table. So you deserve to go out and have a bit of fun.	**Situation 2** **Character B** You are A's parent. Recently A has been lying about homework or brushing teeth. You are worried that there might be bigger issues A might also be lying about. Trust between you and A needs rebuilding. Also you are worried about the influence that some of A's friends are having.
Situation 3 **Character A** At break time you suddenly see how B shouts at a younger student and wants to kick him. You don't know B, but your friend told you that B had been bullying someone when they were in primary school.	**Situation 3** **Character B** For the third time already this week a student one year below you laughed at you and called you names. You didn't do anything. You get really angry and want to show him that he needs to stop. When asking your mum for advice, she told you it was about time you stood up for yourself.

My Challenge

Activity Objective

To define challenges as an opportunity for development and learning.

Intended Audience

Individual, pairs

Context

This activity encourages students to develop a positive attitude towards challenges they face.

Activity Instructions

1) Discuss which challenges the student(s) have faced in the past. Let each student pick out one in their mind that they have successfully mastered.

2) Now look at Activity Sheet 14 together. A challenge can sometimes feel like a mountain to climb. It takes determination and hard work to overcome difficulties. When having achieved a difficult task, it is important that we come away stronger and with the feeling that this helped us to further develop our personality.

3) Ask the student(s) to look more closely at the challenge they have in their mind from the past using Activity Sheet 15.

4) Look at the completed grid together and let each student explain it further. Try to work out what helped them to overcome the challenge (e.g. taking advice from parent/teacher/friend or their own determination). Concentrate on talking about the feelings the student had after his/her success.

Closing the Activity

Draw the activity to a close by reminding the student(s) of their feelings when successfully completing a challenge they have faced and sum up what exactly had helped them.

14 **Activity Sheet**

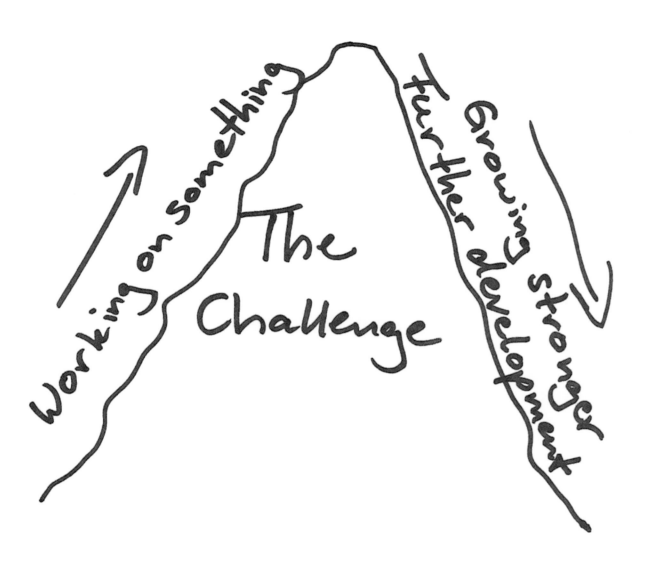

Working on something

The Challenge

Growing stronger

Further development

Activity Sheet

Describe briefly what your challenge was about.	
What did you do to tackle the challenge?	
How did you feel afterwards?	
What helped you to master the challenge?	

The Rushing River

Activity Objective
The students practise working together as a group. They have to focus on getting all students across an imagined river rather than just themselves.

Intended Audience
Groups of at least six students up to whole class size

Context
This activity is a challenge from adventure pedagogy. The members of the group learn to look after each other and experience that their steps have consequences for the whole group. Success is only possible together.

Activity Instructions
1. Set up the activity using Activity Sheet 16 as an overview. Use whatever you have – for the starting and finishing line you can use masking tape, a rope or ideally long gym benches. The 'stones' can be wooden planks/pieces of carpet/newspaper etc. Make sure that the distance between the lines is wide enough so the students will have to use all four 'stones' to get across. Put the four 'stones' at the starting line.
2. When the students arrive, explain the setup and the aim of the activity to the group. An imaginary fast-flowing river has to be crossed with the help of four 'stones' that they can put down into the river. If they lose contact with one of the stones it gets washed away – the instructor takes it away quickly – and crossing becomes impossible. Can they manage to look after each other so well that everyone gets across? If one of them falls into the river or they lose a stone the whole group will have to restart the activity.
3. No matter if the group manages the activity well or not – feel free to stop the activity in between to mirror to the group how they are working together. You can also use one student to be the 'spectator' and reflect to the group what he/she can see. What is working? What does the group still need in order to be able to achieve the task?
4. Variation: With a bigger group you can make two teams and have a competition. You will need four more 'stones'. Which team gets across quicker? Analyse together with the students: What helped this team to work together effectively and look after each other?

Closing the Activity
Stand in a circle and let each member of the group say what they gained from this activity. Where possible help the students to transfer their findings into everyday life situations.

Activity Sheet

The Rushing River

Below is an outline showing the setting for the activity

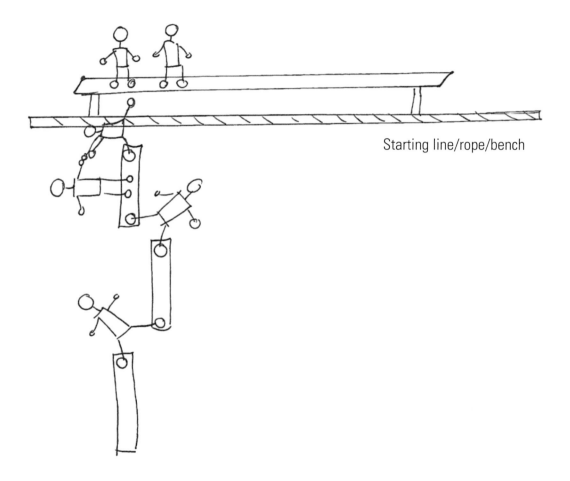

Starting line/rope/bench

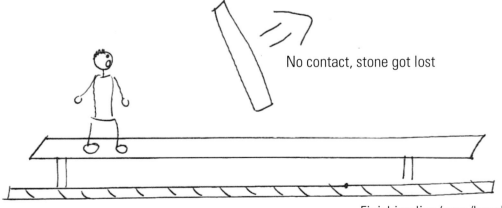

No contact, stone got lost

Finishing line/rope/bench

My Place of Strength

Activity Objective

Working with symbols and inner pictures is a very powerful tool in strengthening a student's character. The activity helps students to find their inner place of peace.

Intended Audience

Individual and groups up to class size

Context

In this activity students develop a picture and a feeling for an inner place of peace and strength. Using their imagination they can explore and get to know their own personal place of strength and learn to use this image when facing trouble.

Activity Instructions

1. Ask the student(s) to just go along with this activity and to take it seriously. Invite them to start travelling on an inner journey. Place colouring pencils and unlined paper next to each student.

2. Let each student find a comfortable position that they can stay in for about 15 minutes. If you are in a large enough space they can sit or lie on the floor; if not, sitting comfortably on a chair works fine too.

3. Ask the student(s) to close their eyes. Wait for a few moments until the room is completely calm.

4. Using Activity Sheet 17 read the story out slowly. Make sure everyone can hear you well. Pause where you think it needs time for the image to develop in the students' imagination.

    If you repeat this activity, you can add more aspects to it. For example, the student(s) go with a backpack filled with their worries and they unpack it in their place of safety and leave the things behind, being taken care of in their inner place. To the story you can add animals as figures to identify with, dwarves or elves as helpers or Sophia the lady of wisdom. Use your own imagination and maybe find some information about dream journeys to develop this activity further if your students are receptive to it.

5. At the end of the story have a few moments of silence to let the student(s) arrive back in the room. Ask them to open their eyes again and remain silent.

6. Without speaking to each other the student(s) now use the colouring pencils to draw their place that they have seen in their imagination as the place most important for them. It can be in the meadow, forest, sun, sky, rock, river, source, lake or whatever detail they found most important for themselves in the story. Encourage the student(s) to just start and let their picture develop. There is no right or wrong, no "But I can't draw" and no commenting on other students' drawings. Each picture only gives meaning for the one who draws it.

7. After they have finished drawing, explain the purpose of this activity. They have now visited a place in their imagination where they feel comfortable and strong. Ask them to go there with their inner eye at least once a day, so they get to know it well and learn to access it easily. When they feel stressed or sad or angry – any strong emotions that they can't live out at the moment – they can use their imagination to visit their inner place of strength to gain control and comfort in the situation. When the storm rises around them they can find calmness inside.

Closing the Activity

Close the activity without feedback or exchange this time. Let the story and drawing work without breaking it with many further words. Let the student(s) take their drawing home with them.

In a following session ask the student(s) about their inner place. Have they managed to visit it? Have they used it as a place of strength when in trouble? Do they want to give feedback on the activity? Do they have any questions?

Journey of Strength

Find a comfortable position where you can be still for about 10 minutes. Close your eyes and let your breath flow in and out of your mouth easily. Allow yourself to relax.

Using your imagination you get up, go to the door and leave the room. Outside you find that there is no hard corridor floor. The ground has turned into green grass. You bend down to touch it. It is soft and still a little wet from the morning dew. When you get up again, the walls are now trees lining the meadow you stand on. You can see the sun rising up behind the trees. You look around. In which direction do you want to go? You choose to go left where you can see many trees. You start walking, then running – faster and faster. You feel full of energy. It is fun to run through the grass, which is getting higher, reaching up to your knees now. You see many colourful flowers in all different shapes rushing past you as you run.

When you arrive at the trees you stop running. It is as if you enter a different room now. It is much darker because of the leaves above you. You look up. The dark green leaves of the trees rustle in a gentle breeze. Slim rays of sunlight shine through the leafy ceiling and dance on your face. You enjoy this for a moment. You stretch out your arms and pretend to be a tree, standing strong with your many branches, where the birds build their nests.

Then you look forward and see the soft, brown forest floor. It smells woody and moist, like moss. You walk without a path, finding your own way between the trunks of the old trees. With each step you sink a little into the ground. There are many layers of past years' leaves underneath you, which is comforting. The seasons come and go and the trees are still here happily growing stronger and stronger. You walk down a slope; the ground becomes even softer, so you can hear your steps squelching in the muddy ground.

A little bit of water comes out of the ground right in front of your feet. You stop and look closer. This water is a source, coming up right here from deep down under the ground. And you have found this place. The water from the source is very cold, but very special in this dark, muddy place. It is washing away the leaves and has made its own way down the slope. Little as it seems it must have a lot of strength – continuing to flow day and night.

You realise that the water of the source is collecting at a pool of rocks and a little river is forming from it. It is quietly mumbling along the forest floor. Here the sun breaks through the forest ceiling and makes the water sparkle. Little, glistening stars play on its surface. You dip your hand into the water. It feels cool, clean and refreshing. You decide to follow the little river. It gets wider and stronger and louder further down. You follow it, sometimes letting a brown leaf float down. The water supports it and guides it on its way.

At the side of the river you notice a huge, grey rock. You touch it. It is hard but not as cold as the water – the sun has been warming it. You climb on to its strong back and ride on it. Looking down you enjoy the view over a valley. There are colourful meadows and a big, calm lake at the end of the valley.

When climbing down the rock on the other side you notice a big hole. It is dark, yet inviting you to have a look. It is big enough for you to slip in. There is little light, but it is dry and safe in here. You smile to yourself and are excited that you found this hiding place inside the big rock. Sitting at the entrance to the cave the sun is warming you. You can see the trees, the meadows and the lake in the valley. You hear the water of the river coming from the source. You feel like you have arrived within yourself. You feel peaceful and happy, watching a few clouds make their way across the sky. You feel how your journey today has made you stronger.

In your mind go back to the place which most fascinated you or where you wanted to stay longer. Try to picture it again in your mind, seeing the colours, touching it, smelling it. Get to know it further.

Then slowly come back and stand in front of the door. When you are ready, open the door and come back to your place. Slowly open your eyes.

The Bounce Back Boat

Activity Objective

To provide a picture of the elements which make up a resilient personality.

Intended Audience

Individual, pairs, small groups

Context

This activity can stand at the beginning of the journey or be taken as a reminder of the areas that we work on.

Activity Instructions

1. Look at the blank boat on Activity Sheet 18 together. Considering what you might need as a base, a mast and sails for coping well under pressure, talk about which elements could be helpful. Fill in the parts of the boat with the help of Activity Sheet 19.

    Sails: vitality, full of life, assertiveness, actively shaping what I work on, following my interests, room for creativity, finding solutions, sense of direction

    Masts: Accepting/loving myself, self-esteem, following what I believe in

    Boat: Acceptance from peers and family, connection to my community, positive inner attitude

2. Talk about the different parts. What do the words mean to you? Do you have examples for situations in your life where you can see these attributes? What is lacking in your life? Is there something that could help you to take steps in this direction?

Closing the Activity

Sum up the main points of your discussion and remind the student(s) of the steps they want to address in the following week. In the next session refer back to these steps and ask about any experiences.

18 Activity Sheet

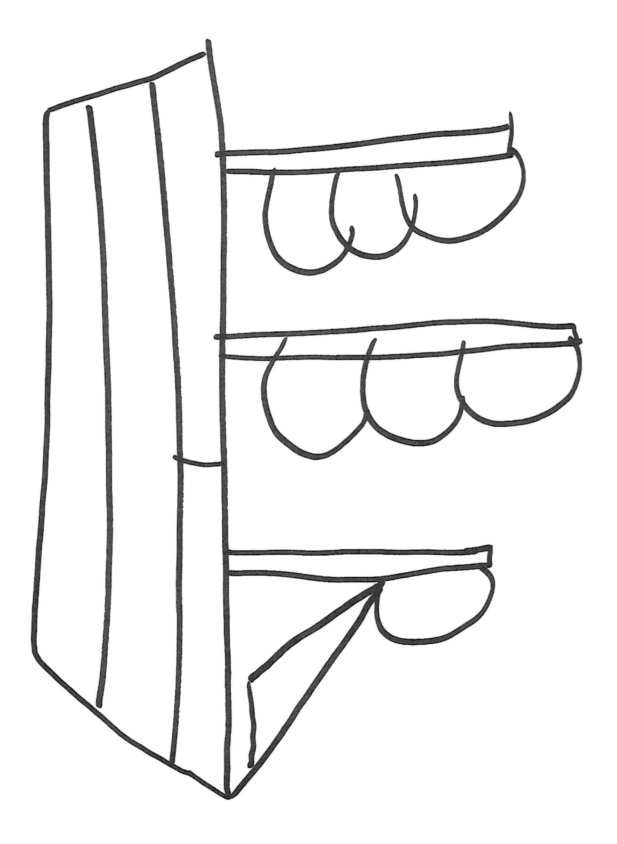

19 Activity Sheet

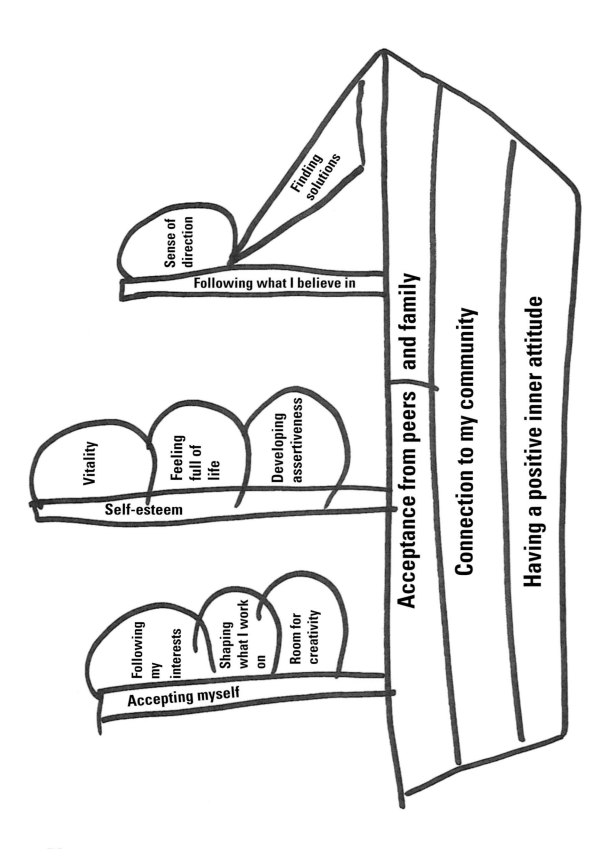

How Bouncy are You?

Activity Objective

To explore topics around flexibility and pressure with a hands-on activity.

Intended Audience

Individual, pairs, small groups

Context

Often it is good to approach a topic with 'head and hands'. This activity allows students to think about flexibility and acting under stress while applying pressure to a material. This will easily trigger their thinking and get them to talk.

Activity Instructions

1. Prepare either different materials like clay, bouncing balls, stress balls, rubber, play dough etc or concentrate on just one of these materials if you think providing more than one will distract the student(s).

2. Ask the student(s) to talk about the material in their hand. Explore topics around flexibility, bouncing back, compensating, pressure, stress etc while handling the material provided. If using more than one material compare how they each react differently to pressure.

3. Ask the student(s) to consider:

    When is it important to be flexible?

    In which situations would you like to react to pressure in a more relaxed way?

    When do you need to take a stand?

    When is it good to be 'hard' - to stand up for something or someone?

4. Use Activity Sheet 20 for the student(s) to write down their findings. If working with a group you can also use a board or flipchart to draw together the students' thoughts rather than working individually on worksheets.

Closing the Activity

Close the activity by summing up the students' findings and ask them to keep their eyes open, looking for example situations that they should bring to the next session. Ask them about their experience next time you see them.

Activity Sheet

When is it important to be flexible?

In which situations would you like to react to pressure in a more relaxed way?

When do you need to take a stand?

When is it good to be 'hard' - to stand up for something or someone?

Do Something for Your Community

Activity Objective

To motivate students to play an active part in their community.

Intended Audience

Individual, pairs and small groups

Context

To develop inner strength a well-functioning community is of great importance. This activity looks at ways the student(s) can get involved in their community.

Activity Instructions

1. Together with the student(s) look at the examples on Activity Sheet 21.

2. Discuss: What will you do? What can you contribute to your school community? Which programmes can you join? How can you make a difference for someone? Find more examples for the empty boxes!

3. Don't just stay in the theoretical discussion. Help the student(s) to set themselves a SMART target for their own community action. Let them pick out one or two personal goals they want to achieve in terms of being active in their community. The SMART target needs to be:

    S – specific, M – measurable, A – achievable, R – realistic, T – time focused.

4. In the next session review where the student(s) got to with their community targets.

Closing the Activity

Draw the activity to an end by pointing out to the student(s) that being part of a community network is fun, good for their health and keeps them active. They are better at empathising with other people, which will help them in their job and later life.

21 Activity Sheet

Do Something for Your Community

Bake or cook something for a friend

Carry your elderly neighbour's shopping home

Do a first-aid course

Join or start a club in your school

Give the people you meet a smile

Find out about volunteering for a cause that interests you – protecting nature, animal rescue, children in poverty…

Play outside, see who is around in your street and ask them to play football or go to the park with you

Tell one of your teachers what you think they are doing very well

The Resilience Choice Card Game

Activity Objective

For students to play a game where they examine certain adjectives and what they mean to them in the context of resilience building.

Intended Audience

Pairs or small groups

Context

This activity helps students to consider a bank of resilience traits and strengths in the format of a game.

Activity Instructions

1. Copy Activity Sheet 22 (Resilience Choice Cards) onto card.

2. Cut out the cards, shuffle them and place them face down.

3. In turns, take a card and turn it over.

4. Discuss how each student is able to demonstrate the quality on the card.

5. Prompt each student to give an example.

6. Develop this activity further by using Activity Sheet 23 to create your own bespoke cards.

Closing the Activity

Close the activity by bringing together the qualities discussed and how they can be further developed by the students.

Resilience Choice Cards

Respectful	Kind	Considerate
Optimistic	Caring	Trustworthy
Courageous	Fair	Responsible
Honest	Forgiving	Patient

Resilience Choice Bespoke Cards

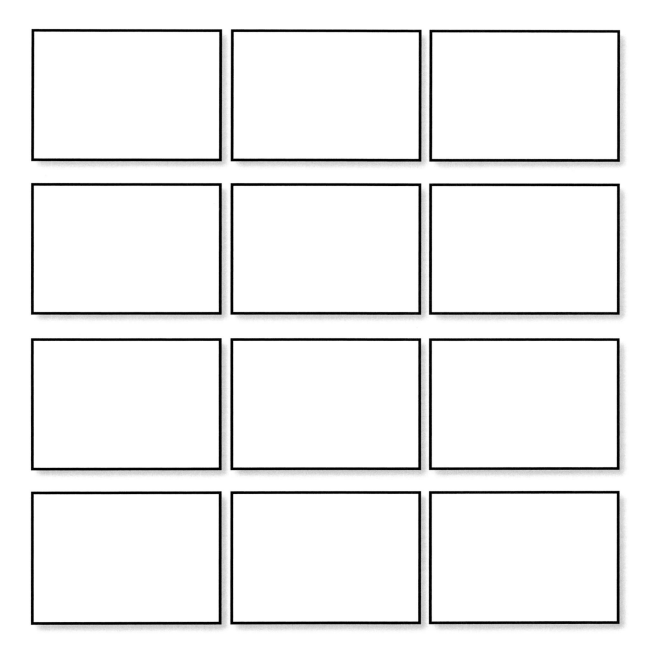

What is This Feeling?

Activity Objective

To give students the opportunity to reflect upon the physical responses to stress.

Intended Audience

Individual

Context

In moments of stress there are physical responses and the flight or fight response is present. This activity gives the student an opportunity to think about where he/she feels stressed and raises awareness of the physical aspects.

Activity Instructions

1)   Lead the student through Activity Sheet 24. Ask the student to note his/her physical responses and reactions.

2)   Lead the student through discussion about this and how he/she might manage these physical reactions.

Closing the Activity

Close the activity by cementing the suggestion of being aware of what physical reactions might occur if the student found him- or herself in a similar situation.

24 Activity Sheet

What happens to your voice?

What happens to your hands?

What happens to your face?

What happens to you inside ?

What happens to your breathing?

25 **Activity Sheet**

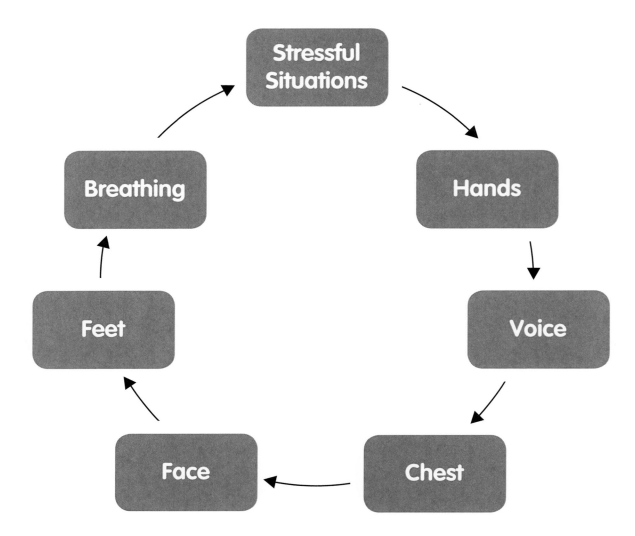

Ways of Coping with Difficult Situations

Activity Objective

For students to generate ways of coping in moments of crisis.

Intended Audience

Individual or small group setting

Context

The busy school environment can trigger some undesirable responses. Here we think about what to do when things start to become challenging.

Activity Instructions

1. Lead a discussion on ways of coping and work through 'Coping Strategies' (Activity Sheet 26).

2. Lead the students through the 'Commitment to Myself' sheet (Activity Sheet 27).

3. Activity Sheet 28 is a prompt sheet to scaffold the learning in this activity that you can use to prompt the student(s).

Closing the Activity

Review with the student(s) where and when they can get help in a crisis or any given situation.

26 Activity Sheet

Coping Strategies – Generating Ways of Coping with Stressful Situations

I might

Maybe I could

Perhaps

27 Activity Sheet

Coping Strategies – Generating Ways of Coping with Stress Prompt Sheet

Meditate	Call a friend	Go for a walk	Take deep breaths
Sing	Dance	Take a bath	Buy yourself some flowers
Make a gift for someone	Go for a run	Rest with your legs up against a wall and your back on the floor	Write a letter to yourself
Light a candle	Start keeping a journal	Cook a healthy meal	Give someone a hug

A Commitment to Myself

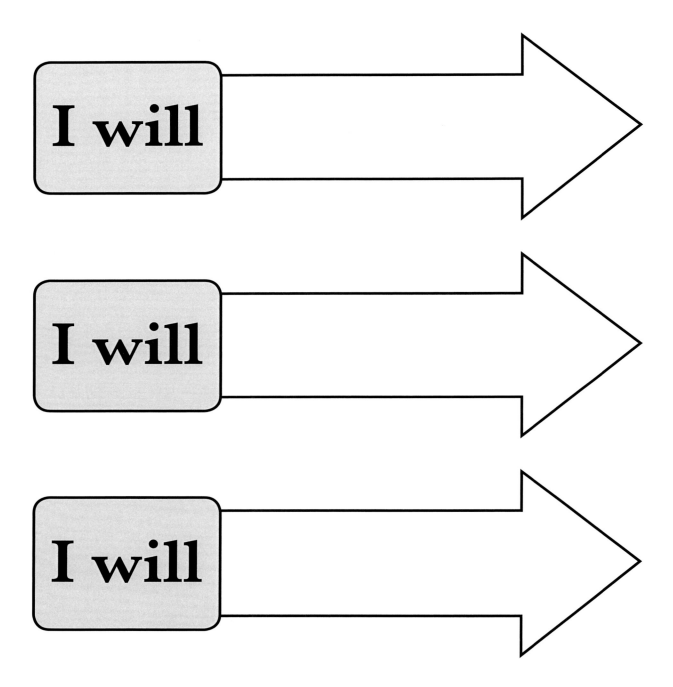

What's That in Your Bag?

Activity Objective

To give students the opportunity to consider a dilemma-based learning situation.

Intended Audience

Individual, small groups

Context

Students are often faced with dilemmas which can be challenging and emotionally charged. This activity helps to develop a range of resilience skills to address these challenges.

Activity Instructions

1. Lead the student(s) through the dilemma (Activity Sheet 29), asking them to consider their responses.

2. Lead the student(s) through the dilemma again, this time asking if there is an alternative way of responding to the situation, thus encouraging further thinking.

Closing the Activity

Close the activity by asking the student(s) to consider what would be the ideal response if they found themselves in a situation of difficulty.

Activity Sheet

What's That in Your Bag? Dilemma

You and your friend are both in year 11.

Your friend is looking tired and appears snappy and short tempered. She appears distracted a lot of the time and when you ask she says that she's finding it hard to cope with the pressure of her GCSE exams and can't seem to concentrate.

You are really worried about her but she does not wish to talk about it.

At school today while looking for her pencil case, some pills fall out of her bag. She quickly puts them back but you think that they are sleeping pills.

She refuses to talk to you about this and tells you not to tell anyone.

What do you do?

I Think She's Hurting Herself

Activity Objective

To give students the opportunity to consider a dilemma-based learning situation.

Intended Audience

Individual, small groups

Context

Students are often faced with dilemmas which can be challenging and emotionally difficult. This activity helps to develop a range of resilience skills to address these challenges.

Activity Instructions

1. Lead the student(s) through the dilemma (Activity Sheet 30), asking them to consider their responses in these challenging scenarios.

    Key question:

    - What would you do? What would you advise a friend to do?

2. Ask the student(s) to create their own dilemma that might be suitable for use with a younger student.

Closing the Activity

Close the activity by reflecting upon the responses and consider when there might be an opportunity to use the activity with a group or pair of younger students.

I Think She's Hurting Herself

A best friend has been having some difficulty with people that she knows making nasty comments on social media.

She has said that she does not want to talk to anyone about this.

You notice that there are some marks on her wrists and she often pulls her sleeves over her fingers. They are red and sore but you are not quite sure exactly what they are. You suspect that she is harming herself.

You are very worried and afraid.

What do you do?

Student Tracking and Evaluation Workbook

Mental Health & Well-Being Activities

Resilience
Coping Strategies

| Student Name: |
| Form: |

How to use this Tracking and Evaluation Workbook

This Workbook can be used to track and evaluate the activities undertaken and the progress made during the resilience sessions. At the end of each activity please use the Workbook to record student progress and evaluate the sessions.

Assess the student's engagement with the process and responses during the sessions. A rating could be applied in terms of evaluation as follows:

1	Student disengaged and activity not completed
2	Student somewhat engaged and activity partially completed
3	Student engaged and made a positive attempt at completing the activities
4	Student fully engaged and activity fully completed

Date completed: (Date of Activity completion)	Activity Title
Student Evaluation (Student to write in their comment)	

Practitioner Assessment & Comment (Circle Rating below)				Comment
1	2	3	4	

Date completed: (Date of Activity completion)	Activity Title
Student Evaluation (Student to write in their comment)	

Practitioner Assessment & Comment (Circle Rating below)				Comment
1	2	3	4	

Date completed: (Date of Activity completion)	Activity Title
Student Evaluation (Student to write in their comment)	

Practitioner Assessment & Comment (Circle Rating below)	Comment

1	2	3	4

Date completed: (Date of Activity completion)	Activity Title
Student Evaluation (Student to write in their comment)	

Practitioner Assessment & Comment (Circle Rating below)	Comment

1	2	3	4

Date completed: (Date of Activity completion)	Activity Title
Student Evaluation (Student to write in their comment)	

Practitioner Assessment & **Comment** (Circle Rating below)				**Comment**
1	2	3	4	

Date completed: (Date of Activity completion)	Activity Title
Student Evaluation (Student to write in their comment)	

Practitioner Assessment & **Comment** (Circle Rating below)				**Comment**
1	2	3	4	

Date completed: (Date of Activity completion)	Activity Title
Student Evaluation (Student to write in their comment)	

Practitioner Assessment & Comment (Circle Rating below)				**Comment**
1	2	3	4	

Date completed: (Date of Activity completion)	Activity Title
Student Evaluation (Student to write in their comment)	

Practitioner Assessment & Comment (Circle Rating below)				**Comment**
1	2	3	4	

Date completed: (Date of Activity completion)	Activity Title
Student Evaluation (Student to write in their comment)	

Practitioner Assessment & Comment (Circle Rating below)				**Comment**
1	2	3	4	

Date completed: (Date of Activity completion)	Activity Title
Student Evaluation (Student to write in their comment)	

Practitioner Assessment & Comment (Circle Rating below)				**Comment**
1	2	3	4	

Date completed: (Date of Activity completion)	Activity Title
Student Evaluation (Student to write in their comment)	

Practitioner Assessment & Comment (Circle Rating below)	Comment

1	2	3	4

Date completed: (Date of Activity completion)	Activity Title
Student Evaluation (Student to write in their comment)	

Practitioner Assessment & Comment (Circle Rating below)	Comment

1	2	3	4

Date completed: (Date of Activity completion)	Activity Title
Student Evaluation (Student to write in their comment)	

Practitioner Assessment & Comment (Circle Rating below)				**Comment**
1	2	3	4	

Date completed: (Date of Activity completion)	Activity Title
Student Evaluation (Student to write in their comment)	

Practitioner Assessment & Comment (Circle Rating below)				**Comment**
1	2	3	4	

Date completed: (Date of Activity completion)	Activity Title
Student Evaluation (Student to write in their comment)	

Practitioner Assessment & Comment (Circle Rating below)	Comment
1 2 3 4	

Date completed: (Date of Activity completion)	Activity Title
Student Evaluation (Student to write in their comment)	

Practitioner Assessment & Comment (Circle Rating below)	Comment
1 2 3 4	

Date completed: (Date of Activity completion)	Activity Title

Student Evaluation (Student to write in their comment)

Practitioner Assessment & Comment (Circle Rating below)	Comment

1	2	3	4

Date completed: (Date of Activity completion)	Activity Title

Student Evaluation (Student to write in their comment)

Practitioner Assessment & Comment (Circle Rating below)	Comment

1	2	3	4

Date completed: (Date of Activity completion)	Activity Title
Student Evaluation (Student to write in their comment)	

Practitioner Assessment & Comment (Circle Rating below)	**Comment**

1	2	3	4	

Date completed: (Date of Activity completion)	Activity Title
Student Evaluation (Student to write in their comment)	

Practitioner Assessment & Comment (Circle Rating below)	**Comment**

1	2	3	4	

Bibliography

Community Links Trust (2004) *Change the World for a Fiver*, Short Books.

Doran, G (1981) 'There's a S.M.A.R.T. Way to Write Management's Goals and Objectives', *Management Review*, Vol. 70, Issue 11, pp. 35-36.

Dweck, C S (2012), *Mindset: How You Can Fulfil Your Potential*, Robinson.

Egan, G (2001), *The Skilled Helper: A Problem-Management and Opportunity-Development Approach to Helping*, Wadsworth.

George, S (2010), *The Learning Mentor Manual*, Sage Publications.

George, S (2016) *The Mentoring Toolkit*, Loggerhead Publishing.

Hattie, J (2008), *Visible Learning*, Routledge.

Hymans, M (2003), *Think Before You Act*, Lucky Duck Publishing.

Maehrlein, K (2012) *Die Bambusstrategie*, Gabal Verlag.

Maslow, A H (2013) *A Theory of Human Motivation*, Wilder Publications.

Mosley, J (2013) *Quality Circle Time in the Secondary School*, Routledge.

Promoting children and young people's emotional health and wellbeing: a whole school and college approach DFE.ef: PHE publications gateway number: 2014825

Rogers, B (2006), *Cracking the Hard Class, Paul Chapman Educational Publishing*, 2nd edition.

Supporting mental health in schools and colleges Ref: ISBN 978-1-78105-756-8, DFE-RR697

Tomsett, J (2017) *This Much I Know About Mind Over Matter ... Improving Mental Health in Our Schools,* Crown House Publishing.

WAWWD Community Interest Company (2008) *Teach your granny to text & other ways to change the world*, Walker Books and Short Books.

https://www.gov.uk/government/publications/framework-of-outcomes-for-young-people

Other Stephanie George Titles from Loggerhead Publishing

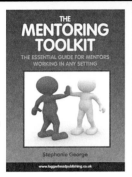